Heart Gifts

Heart Gifts from

Helen Steiner Rice

HUTCHINSON

London Melbourne Sydney Auckland Johannesburg

Hutchinson & Co. (Publishers) Ltd

An imprint of the Hutchinson Publishing Group

17–21 Conway Street, London W1P 6JD

Hutchinson Group (Australia) Pty Ltd
30–32 Cremorne Street, Richmond South, Victoria 3121
PO Box 151, Broadway, New South Wales 2007

Hutchinson Group (NZ) Ltd
32–34 View Road, PO Box 40–086, Glenfield, Auckland 10

Hutchinson Group (SA) (Pty) Ltd
PO Box 337, Bergvlei 2012, South Africa

First published in Great Britain June 1970
Second impression July 1970
Third impression June 1971
Fourth impression April 1972
Fifth impression May 1973
Sixth impression November 1974
Seventh impression November 1976
Eighth impression May 1978
Ninth impression October 1980
Tenth impression October 1981
Eleventh impression October 1982

Printed in Great Britain by The Anchor Press Ltd
and bound by Wm Brendon & Son Ltd
both of Tiptree, Essex

ISBN 0 09 103700 X

CONTENTS

FOREWORD

Show me the way,
        not to fortune and fame,
Not how to win laurels
        or praise for my name—
But Show Me The Way
        to spread "The Great Story"
That "Thine is The Kingdom
        and Power and Glory."

HELEN STEINER RICE

"HEART GIFTS"

It's not the things that can be bought
        that are life's richest treasure,
It's just the little "heart gifts"
        that money cannot measure...
A cheerful smile, a friendly word,
        a sympathetic nod
Are priceless little treasures
        from the storehouse of our God...
They are the things that can't be bought
        with silver or with gold,
For thoughtfulness and kindness
        and love are never sold...
They are the priceless things in life
        for which no one can pay,
And the giver finds rich recompense
        in *giving them away.*

A SURE WAY TO A HAPPY DAY

Happiness is something
      we create in our mind,
It's not something you search for
      and so seldom find—
It's just waking up
      and beginning the day
By counting our blessings
      and kneeling to pray—
It's giving up thoughts
      that breed discontent
And accepting what comes
      as a "gift heaven-sent"—
It's giving up wishing
      for things we have not
And making the best of
      whatever we've got—
It's knowing that life
      is determined for us,
And pursuing our tasks
      without fret, fume or fuss—
For it's by completing
      what God gives us to do
That we find real contentment
      and happiness, too.

PRAYERS ARE THE STAIRS TO GOD

Prayers are the stairs
We must climb every day,
If we would reach God
There is no other way,
For we learn to know God
When we meet Him in prayer
And ask Him to lighten
Our burden of care—
So start in the morning
And, though the way's steep,
Climb ever upward
'Til your eyes close in sleep—
For prayers are the stairs
That lead to the Lord,
And to meet Him in prayer
Is the climber's reward.

THERE'S SUNSHINE IN A SMILE

Life is a mixture
         of sunshine and rain,
Laughter and pleasure,
         teardrops and pain,
All days can't be bright,
         but it's certainly true,
There was never a cloud
         the sun didn't shine through—
So just keep on smiling
         whatever betide you,
Secure in the knowledge
         God is always beside you,
And you'll find when you smile
         your day will be brighter
And all of your burdens
         will seem so much lighter—
For each time you smile
         you will find it is true
Somebody, somewhere
         will *smile back at you,*
And nothing on earth
         can make life more worthwhile
Than the sunshine and warmth
         of a *beautiful smile.*

WIDEN MY VISION

God open my eyes
     so I may see
And feel Your presence
     close to me...
Give me strength
     for my stumbling feet
As I battle the crowd
     on life's busy street,
And widen the vision
     of my unseeing eyes
So in passing faces
     I'll recognize
Not just a stranger,
     unloved and unknown,
But a friend with a heart
     that is much like my own...
Give me perception
     to make me aware
That scattered profusely
     on life's thoroughfare
Are the best *Gifts of God*
     that we daily pass by
As we look at the world
     with an *unseeing eye.*

ANYWHERE IS A PLACE OF PRAYER
IF GOD IS THERE

I have prayed on my knees in the morning,
I have prayed as I walked along,
I have prayed in the silence and darkness
And I've prayed to the tune of a song—
I have prayed in the midst of triumph
And I've prayed when I suffered defeat,
I have prayed on the sands of the seashore
Where the waves of the ocean beat—
I have prayed in a velvet-hushed forest
Where the quietness calmed my fears,
I have prayed through suffering and heartache
When my eyes were blinded with tears—
I have prayed in churches and chapels,
Cathedrals and synagogues, too,
But often I've had the feeling
That my prayers were not getting through,
And I realized then that our Father
Is not really concerned where we pray

Or impressed by our manner of worship
Or the eloquent words that we say ...
He is only concerned with our feelings,
And He looks deep into our heart
And hears the "cry of our soul's deep need"
That no words could ever impart ...
So it isn't the prayer that's expressive
Or offered in some special spot,
It's the sincere plea of a sinner
And God can tell whether or not
We honestly seek His forgiveness
And earnestly mean what we say,
And then and then only He answers
The prayer that we fervently pray.

WHERE CAN WE FIND HIM?

Where can we find *the Holy One?*
Where can we see *His Only Son?*
The Wise Men asked, and we're asking still,
*Where Can We Find This Man of Good
    Will?*
Is He far away in some distant place,
Ruling unseen from His throne of grace?
Is there nothing on earth that man can see
To give him proof of *Eternity?*
It's true we have never looked on His face,
But His likeness shines forth from every place,
For *The Hand of God* is everywhere
Along life's busy thoroughfare...
And His presence can be felt and seen
Right in the midst of our daily routine,
The things we touch and see and feel
Are what make God so very real...
The silent stars in timeless skies,
The wonderment in children's eyes,
The gossamer wings of a humming bird,
The joy that comes from a kindly word...
The autumn haze, the breath of spring,
The chirping song the crickets sing,

A rosebud in a slender vase,
A smile upon a friendly face...
In everything both great and small
We see *the Hand of God in All,*
And every day, somewhere, someplace,
We see *the Likeness of His Face...*
For who can watch a new day's birth
Or touch the warm, life-giving earth,
Or feel the softness of the breeze
Or look at skies through lacy trees
And say they've never seen His face
Or looked upon His throne of grace!

GOD IS NEVER BEYOND OUR REACH

No one ever sought the Father
And found *He* was not *there,*
And no burden is too heavy
To be lightened by a prayer,
No problem is too intricate
And no sorrow that we face
Is too deep and devastating
To be softened by His grace,
No trials and tribulations
Are beyond what we can bear
If we share them with *Our Father*
As we talk to *Him* in prayer—
And men of every colour,
Every race and every creed
Have but to seek the Father
In their deepest hour of need—
God asks for no credentials,
He accepts us with our flaws,
He is kind and understanding
And He welcomes us because
We are His erring children
And He loves us everyone,
And He freely and completely
Forgives all that we have done,
Asking only if we're ready
To follow *where He leads*—
Content that in His wisdom
He will answer all our needs.

GOD'S JEWELS

We watch the rich and famous
Bedecked in precious jewels,
Enjoying earthly pleasures,
Defying moral rules—
And in our mood of discontent
We sink into despair
And long for earthly riches
And feel cheated of our share—
But stop these idle musings,
God has stored up for you
Treasures that are far beyond
Earth's jewels and riches, too—
For never, never discount
What God has promised man
If he will walk in meekness
And accept God's flawless plan—
For if we heed His teachings
As we journey through the years,
We'll find the richest jewels of all
Are *crystalized* from *tears*.

THE PEACE OF MEDITATION

So we may know God better
And feel His quiet power,
Let us daily keep in silence
A *meditation hour*—
For to understand God's greatness
And to use His gifts each day
The soul must learn to meet Him
In a meditative way,
For our Father tells His children
That if they would know His will
They must seek Him in the silence
When all is calm and still...
For nature's greatest forces
Are found in quiet things
Like softly falling snowflakes
Drifting down on angels' wings,
Or petals dropping soundlessly
From a lovely full-blown rose,
So God comes closest to us
When our souls are in repose...
So let us plan with prayerful care
To always allocate
A certain portion of each day
To be still and meditate...
For when everything is quiet

And we're lost in meditation,
Our soul is then preparing
For a deeper dedication
That will make it wholly possible
To quietly endure
The violent world around us—
For in God we are secure.

THANK GOD FOR LITTLE THINGS

Thank you, God, for little things
       that often come our way—
The things we take for granted
       but don't mention when we pray—
The unexpected courtesy,
       the thoughtful, kindly deed—
A hand reached out to help us
       in the time of sudden need—
Oh make us more aware, dear God,
       of little daily graces
That come to us with "sweet surprise"
       from never-dreamed-of places.

STOP SUPPOSIN'

Don't start your day by supposin'
      that trouble is just ahead,
It's better to stop supposin'
      and start with a prayer instead,
And make it a prayer of *Thanksgiving*
      for the wonderful things God has wrought
Like the beautiful sunrise and sunset,
      "God's Gifts" that are free
      and not bought—
For what is the use of supposin'
      the dire things that could happen to you
And worry about some misfortune
      that seldom if ever comes true—
But instead of just idle supposin'
      step forward to meet each new day
Secure in the knowledge God's near you
      to lead you each step of the way—
For supposin' the worst things will happen
      only helps to make them come true
And you darken the bright, happy moments
      that the dear Lord has given to you—
So if you desire to be happy
      and get rid of the *"misery of dread"*
Just give up *"Supposin' the worst things"*
      and look for *"the best things"* instead.

IN HOURS OF DISCOURAGEMENT
GOD IS OUR ENCOURAGEMENT

Sometimes we feel uncertain
And unsure of everything,
Afraid to make decisions,
Dreading what the day will bring—
We keep wishing it were possible
To dispel all fear and doubt
And to understand more readily
Just what life is all about—
God has given us the answers
Which too often go unheeded,
But if we search His promises
We'll find everything that's needed
To lift our faltering spirits
And renew our courage, too,
For there's absolutely nothing
Too much for God to do—
For the Lord is our salvation
And our strength in every fight,
Our redeemer and protector,
Our eternal guiding light—
He has promised to sustain us,
He's our refuge from all harms,

And underneath this refuge
Are the everlasting arms—
So cast your burden on Him,
Seek His counsel when distressed,
And go to Him for comfort
When you're lonely and oppressed—
For God is our encouragement
In trouble and in trials,
And in suffering and in sorrow
He will turn our tears to smiles.

NEVER BORROW SORROW FROM TOMORROW

Deal only with the present,
Never step into tomorrow,
For God asks us just to trust Him
And to never borrow sorrow—
For the future is not ours to know
And it may never be,
So let us live and give our best
And give it lavishly—
For to meet tomorrow's troubles
Before they are even ours
Is to anticipate the Saviour
And to doubt His all-wise powers—
So let us be content to solve
Our problems one by one,
Asking nothing of tomorrow
Except *"Thy Will be done."*

TROUBLE IS A STEPPING-STONE TO GROWTH

Trouble is something no one can escape,
Everyone has it in some form or shape—
Some people hide it way down deep inside,
Some people bear it with gallant-like pride,
Some people worry and complain of their lot,
Some people covet what they haven't got,
While others rebel and become bitter and old
With hopes that are dead and hearts that are cold...
But the wise man accepts whatever God sends,
Willing to yield like a storm-tossed tree bends,
Knowing that God never makes a mistake,
So whatever He sends they are willing to take—
For trouble is part and parcel of life
And no man can grow without trouble and strife,
And the steep hills ahead and high mountain peaks
Afford man at last the peace that he seeks—
So blest are the people who learn to accept
The trouble men try to escape and reject,
For in *our acceptance*
    we're given great grace
And courage and faith and the strength to face
The daily troubles that come to us all
So we may learn to stand "straight and tall"—
For the grandeur of life is born of defeat
For in overcoming we make life complete.

UNAWARE, WE PASS "HIM" BY

On life's busy thoroughfares
We meet with *angels* unawares—
But we are too busy to listen or hear,
Too busy to sense that God is near,
Too busy to stop and recognize
The grief that lies in another's eyes,
Too busy to offer to help or share,
Too busy to sympathize or care,
Too busy to do the *good things* we should,
Telling ourselves we would if we could ...
But life is too swift and the pace is too great
And we dare not pause for we might be late
For our next appointment which means so much,
We are willing to brush off the Saviour's touch,
And we tell ourselves there will come a day
We will have more time to pause on our way ...
But before we know it "life's sun has set"
And we've passed the Saviour but never met,
For hurrying along life's thoroughfare
We passed Him by and remained unaware
That within the *very sight of our eye,*
Unnoticed, the Son of God passed by.

WHEN TROUBLE COMES AND THINGS GO WRONG!

Let us go quietly to God
      when troubles come to us,
Let us never stop to whimper
      or complain and fret and fuss,
Let us hide "our thorns" in "roses"
      and our sighs in "golden song"
And "our crosses" in a "crown of smiles"
      whenever things go wrong...
For no one can really help us
      as our troubles we bemoan,
For *comfort, help* and *inner peace*
      must come from God alone...
So do not tell your neighbour,
      your companion or your friend
In the hope that they can help you
      bring your troubles to an end...
For they, too, have their problems,
      they are burdened just like you,
So *take your cross to Jesus*
      and *He will see you through*...
And waste no time in crying
      on the shoulder of a friend
But go directly to the Lord
      for on Him you can depend...
For there's absolutely *nothing*
      that His mighty hand can't do
And He never is too busy
      to help and comfort you.

FATHERS ARE WONDERFUL PEOPLE

Fathers are wonderful people
    too little understood,
And we do not sing their praises
    as often as we should...
For, somehow, Father seems to be
    the man who pays the bills,
While Mother binds up little hurts
    and nurses all our ills...
And Father struggles daily
    to live up to *"his image"*
As protector and provider
    and "hero of the scrimmage"...
And perhaps that is the reason
    we sometimes get the notion
That Fathers are not subject
    to the thing we call emotion,
But if you look inside Dad's heart,
    where no one else can see,
You'll find he's sentimental
    and as "soft" as he can be...
But he's so busy every day
    in the gruelling race of life,
He leaves the sentimental stuff
    to his partner and his wife...

But Fathers are just *wonderful*
　　　　in a million different ways,
And they merit loving compliments
　　　　and accolades of praise,
For the only reason Dad aspires
　　　　to fortune and success
Is to make the family proud of him
　　　　and to bring them happiness...
And like *Our Heavenly Father,*
　　　　he's a guardian and a guide,
Someone that we can count on
　　　　to be *always on our side.*

A TRIBUTE TO ALL DAUGHTERS

Every home should have a daughter,
        for there's nothing like a girl
To keep the world around her
        in one continuous whirl ...
From the moment she arrives on earth,
        and on through womanhood,
A daughter is a *female*
        who is seldom understood ...
One minute she is laughing,
        the next she starts to cry,
Man just can't understand her
        and there's just no use to try ...
She is soft and sweet and cuddly,
        but she's also wise and smart,
She's a wondrous combination
        of a mind and brain and heart ...
And even in her baby days
        she's just a born coquette,
And anything she really wants
        she manages to get ...
For even at a tender age
        she uses all her wiles
And she can melt the hardest heart
        with the sunshine of her smiles ...
She starts out as a rosebud
        with her beauty unrevealed,
Then through a happy childhood
        her petals are unsealed ...

She's soon a sweet girl graduate,
      and then a blushing bride,
And then a lovely woman
      as the rosebud opens wide...
And some day in the future,
      if it be God's gracious will,
She, too, will be a Mother
      and know that reverent thrill
That comes to every Mother
      whose heart is filled with love
When she beholds the "angel"
      that God sent her from above...
And there would be no life at all
      in this world or the other
Without a *darling daughter*
      who, in turn, becomes a *Mother!*

A PRAYER FOR THE YOUNG
AND LOVELY

Dear God, I keep praying
For the things I desire,
You tell me I'm selfish
And "playing with fire"—
It is hard to believe
I am selfish and vain,
My desires seem so real
And my needs seem so sane,
And yet You are wiser
And Your vision is wide
And You look down on me
And You see deep inside,
You know it's so easy
To change and distort,
And things that are evil
Seem so harmless a sport—
Oh, teach me, dear God,
To not rush ahead
But to pray for Your guidance
And to trust You instead,

For You know what I need
And that I'm only a slave
To the things that I want
And desire and crave—
Oh, God, in your mercy
Look down on me now
And see in my heart
That I love you somehow,
Although in my rashness,
Impatience and greed
I pray for the things
That I *want* and *don't need*—
And instead of a *crown*
Please send me a *cross*
And teach me to know
That *all Gain* is but *loss,*
And show me the way
To joy without end,
With You as my *Father,*
Redeemer and *Friend*—
And send me the things
That are hardest to bear,
And keep me forever
Safe in Thy care.

"THIS TOO WILL PASS AWAY"

If I can endure for this minute
Whatever is happening to me,
No matter how heavy my heart is
Or how "dark" the moment may be—
If I can remain calm and quiet
With all my world crashing about me,
Secure in the knowledge God loves me
When everyone else seems to doubt me—
If I can but keep on believing
What I know in my heart to be true,
That "darkness will fade with the morning"
And that *this will pass away, too*—
Then nothing in life can defeat me
For as long as this knowledge remains
I can suffer whatever is happening
For I know God will break "all the chains"
That are binding me tight in *"the Darkness"*
And trying to fill me with fear—
For there is *no night without dawning*
And I know that *"my morning"* is near.

MORE OF THEE ... LESS OF ME

Take me and break me and make me, dear God,
Just what you want me to be—
Give me the strength to accept what you send
And eyes with the vision to see
All the small arrogant ways that I have
And the vain little things that I do,
Make me aware that I'm often concerned
More with *myself* than with *You,*
Uncover before me my weakness and greed
And help me to search deep inside
So I may discover how easy it is
To be selfishly lost in my pride—
And then in Thy goodness and mercy
Look down on this weak, erring one
And tell me that I am forgiven
For all I've so willfully done,
And teach me to humbly start following
The path that the dear Saviour trod
So I'll find at the end of life's journey
"A Home in the city of God."

WARM OUR HEARTS WITH THY LOVE

Oh, God, who made the summer
        and warmed the earth with beauty,
Warm our hearts with gratitude
        and devotion to our duty,
For in this age of violence,
        rebellion and defiance
We've forgotten the true meaning
        of "dependable reliance"—
We have lost our sense of duty
        and our sense of values, too,
And what was once unsanctioned,
        no longer is taboo,
Our standards have been lowered
        and we resist all discipline,
And our vision has been narrowed
        and blinded to all sin—
Oh, put the summer brightness
        in our closed, unseeing eyes
So in the careworn faces
        that we pass we'll recognize
The heartbreak and the loneliness,
        the trouble and despair
That a word of understanding
        would make easier to bear—
Oh, God, look down on our cold hearts
        and warm them with Your love,
And grant us Your forgiveness
        which we're so unworthy of.

NO PRAYER GOES UNHEARD

Often we pause and wonder
When we kneel down to pray—
Can God really hear
The prayers that we say ...
But if we keep praying
And talking to *Him,*
He'll brighten the soul
That was clouded and dim,
And as we continue
Our burden seems lighter,
Our sorrow is softened
And our outlook is brighter—
For though we feel helpless
And alone when we start,
Our prayer is the key
That opens the heart,
And as our heart opens
The dear Lord comes in
And the prayer that we felt
We could never begin
Is so easy to say
For the Lord understands
And gives us new strength
By the touch of His hands.

DAILY PRAYERS DISSOLVE YOUR CARES

I meet God in the morning
And go with Him through the day,
Then in the stillness of the night
Before sleep comes I pray
That God will just "take over"
All the problems I couldn't solve
And in the peacefulness of sleep
My cares will all dissolve,
So when I open up my eyes
To greet another day
I'll find myself renewed in strength
And there'll open up a way
To meet what seemed impossible
For me to solve alone
And once again I'll be assured
I am never *"on my own"*...
For if we try to stand alone
We are weak and we will fall,
For God is always *Greatest*
When we're helpless, lost and small,
And no day is unmeetable
If on rising our first thought
Is to thank God for the blessings
That His loving care has brought...

For there can be no failures
Or hopeless, unsaved sinners
If we enlist the help of God
Who makes all losers winners...
So meet Him in the morning
And go with Him through the day
And thank Him for His guidance
Each evening when you pray,
And if you follow faithfully
This daily way to pray
You will never in your lifetime
Face another "hopeless day."

BEFORE YOU CAN DRY ANOTHER'S TEARS — YOU TOO MUST WEEP!

Let me not live a life that's free
From *"the things"* that draw me close to *Thee*—
For how can I ever hope to heal
The wounds of others I do not feel—
If my eyes are dry and I never weep,
How do I know when the hurt is deep—
If my heart is cold and it never bleeds,
How can I tell what my brother needs—
For when ears are deaf to the beggar's plea
And we close our eyes and refuse to see,
And we steel our hearts and harden our mind,
And we count it a weakness whenever we're kind,
We are no longer following *the Father's Way*
Or seeking His guidance from day to day—
For, without "crosses to carry" and "burdens to bear,"
We dance through a life that is frothy and fair,
And "chasing the rainbow" we have no desire
For "roads that are rough" and "realms that are higher"—
So spare me no heartache or sorrow, dear Lord,
For the heart that is hurt reaps the richest reward,
And God enters the heart that is broken with sorrow
As He opens the door to a *Brighter Tomorrow,*
For only through tears can we recognize
The suffering that lies in another's eyes.

GOD, GIVE US "DRIVE" BUT KEEP US FROM BEING "DRIVEN"

There's a difference between "drive" and "driven"—
The one is selfish the other God-given—
For the "driven man" has but one goal,
Just worldly wealth and not "riches of soul,"
And daily he's spurred on to reach and attain
A higher position, more profit and gain,
Ambition and wealth become his great need
As daily he's "driven" by avarice and greed...
But most blessed are they who use their "drive"
To work with zeal so all men may survive,
For while they forfeit great personal gain
Their work and their zeal are never in vain...
For they contribute to the whole human race
And we cannot survive without growing in grace,
So help us, dear God, to choose between
The "driving force" that rules our routine
So we may make our purpose and goal
Not power and wealth but the growth of our soul...
And give us *strength* and *drive* and *desire*
To raise our standards and ethics higher
So all of Us and not *just a few*
May live on earth...*as You want Us to.*

THE WAY TO GOD

If my days were untroubled
    and my heart always light
Would I seek that fair land
    where there is no night;
If I never grew weary
    with the weight of my load
Would I search for God's Peace
    at the end of the road;
If I never knew sickness
    and never felt pain
Would I reach for a hand
    to help and sustain;
If I walked not with sorrow
    and lived without loss
Would my soul seek sweet solace
    at the foot of the cross;
If all I desired was mine
    day by day
Would I kneel before God
    and earnestly pray;

If God sent no "Winter"
        to freeze me with fear
Would I yearn for the warmth
        of "Spring" every year;
I ask myself this
        and the answer is plain—
If my life were all pleasure
        and I never knew pain
I'd seek God less often
        and need Him much less,
For God's sought more often
        in times of distress,
And no one knows God
        or sees Him as plain
As those who have met Him
        on "The Pathway of Pain."

PRAYERS CAN'T BE ANSWERED
UNLESS THEY ARE PRAYED

Life without purpose
        is barren indeed—
There can't be a harvest
        unless you plant seed,
There can't be attainment
        unless there's a goal,
And man's but a robot
        unless there's a soul...
If we send no ships out,
        no ships will come in,
And unless there's a contest,
        nobody can win...
For games can't be won
        unless they are played,
And *Prayers* can't be *answered*
        unless they are *prayed*...
So whatever is wrong
        with your life today,

You'll find a solution
    if you kneel down and pray
Not just for pleasure,
    enjoyment and health,
Not just for honors
    and prestige and wealth...
But *Pray for a Purpose*
    to *make life worth living,*
And *Pray for the Joy*
    of *unselfish giving,*
For *Great is your Gladness*
    and *Rich your Reward*
When you make your *Life's Purpose*
    the choice of the Lord.

GOD BLESS AMERICA

"America the beautiful"—
May it always stay that way—
But to keep *"Old Glory"* flying
There's a price that we must pay . . .
For everything worth having
Demands work and sacrifice,
And *freedom* is a *Gift* from *God*
That commands the *highest price* . . .
For all our wealth and progress
Are as worthless as can be
Without the *Faith* that made us great
And kept *our country free* . . .
Nor can our nation hope to live
Unto itself alone,
For the problems of our neighbors
Must today become our own . . .
And while it's hard to understand
The complexities of war,
Each one of us must realize
That we are fighting for
The principles of freedom
And the decency of man,
And as a Christian Nation
We're committed to God's Plan . . .

And as the *Land* of *Liberty*
And a great God-fearing nation
We must protect our honor
And fulfill our obligation...
So in these times of crisis
Let us offer no resistance
In giving help to those who need
Our strength and our assistance—
And *"The Stars and Stripes Forever"*
Will remain a symbol of
A rich and mighty nation
Built on *Faith* and *Truth* and *Love.*

COUNT YOUR GAINS AND
NOT YOUR LOSSES

As we travel down life's busy road
Complaining of our heavy load,
We often think God's been unfair
And gave us much more than our share
Of little daily irritations
And disappointing tribulations...
We're discontented with our lot
And all the "bad breaks" that we got,
We count our losses, not our gain,
And remember only tears and pain...
The good things we forget completely
When God looked down and blessed us sweetly,
Our troubles fill our every thought,
We dwell upon lost goals we sought,
And wrapped up in our own despair
We have no time to see or share
Another's load that far outweighs
Our little problems and dismays...
And so we walk with head held low
And little do we guess or know
That someone near us on life's street
Is burdened deeply with defeat...
But if we'd but forget *our care*
And stop in sympathy to share
The burden that "our brother" carried,
Our mind and heart would be less harried
And we would feel our load was small,
In fact, *we carried no load at all.*

EVERYWHERE ACROSS THE LAND YOU SEE GOD'S FACE AND TOUCH HIS HAND

Each time you look up in the sky
Or watch the fluffy clouds drift by,
Or feel the sunshine warm and bright,
Or watch the dark night turn to light,
Or hear a bluebird gayly sing,
Or see the winter turn to spring,
Or stop to pick a daffodil,
Or gather violets on some hill . . .
Or touch a leaf or see a tree,
It's all *God* whispering *"This Is Me . . .*
And *I am Faith* and *I am Light*
And *in Me there shall be no night."*

GOD KNOWS BEST

Our Father knows what's best for us,
So why should we complain—
We always want the sunshine,
But He knows there must be rain—
We love the sound of laughter
And the merriment of cheer,
But our hearts would lose their tenderness
If we never shed a tear...
Our Father tests us often
With suffering and with sorrow,
He tests us, not to punish us,
But to help us meet *tomorrow*...
For growing trees are strengthened
When they withstand the storm,
And the sharp cut of the chisel
Gives the marble grace and form...
God never hurts us needlessly,
And He never wastes our pain,
For every loss He sends to us
Is followed by rich gain...
And when we count the blessings
That God has so freely sent,

We will find no cause for murmuring
And no time to lament...
For Our Father loves His children,
And to Him all things are plain,
So He never sends us *pleasure*
When the *soul's deep need is pain*...
So whenever we are troubled,
And when everything goes wrong,
It is just God working in us
To make *our spirit strong.*

BLESSINGS IN DISGUISE ARE
DIFFICULT TO RECOGNIZE

God sends His "little angels"
        in many forms and guises,
They come as lovely miracles
        that God alone devises—
For He does nothing without purpose,
        everything's a perfect plan
To fulfill in bounteous measure
        all He ever promised man—
For every "little angel"
        with a body bent and broken,
Or a little mind retarded
        or little words unspoken,
Is just God's way of trying
        to reach and touch the hand
Of all who do not know Him
        and cannot understand
That often through an angel
        whose "wings will never fly"
The Lord is pointing out the way
        to His eternal sky
Where there will be no handicaps
        of body, soul or mind,
And where all limitations
        will be dropped and left behind—
So accept these "little angels"
        as gifts from God above
And thank Him for this lesson
        in *Faith* and *Hope* and *Love.*

BIRTHDAYS ARE A GIFT
FROM GOD

Where does *time* go in its endless flight—
Spring turns to fall and day to night,
And birthdays come and birthdays go
And where they go we do not know...
But God who planned our life on earth
And gave our mind and body birth
And then enclosed a living soul
With heaven as the spirit's goal
Has given man the gift of choice
To follow that small inner voice
That speaks to us from year to year
Reminding us we've naught to fear...
For *birthdays* are a *steppingstone*
To endless joys as yet unknown,
So fill each day with happy things
And may your burdens all take wings
And fly away and leave behind
Great joy of heart and peace of mind...
For *birthdays* are *the gateway* to
An *endless life of joy for you*
If you but pray from day to day
That He will show you the *Truth* and
      The Way.

MY GOD IS NO STRANGER

I've never seen God,
  but I know how I feel...
It's people like *you*
  who make *Him "so real"*...
My God is no stranger,
  He's friendly and gay...
And *He* doesn't ask me
  to weep when I pray...
It seems that I pass *Him*
  so often each day...
In the faces of people
  I meet on my way...
He's the stars in the heaven,
  a smile on some face...
A leaf on a tree
  or a rose in a vase...
He's winter and autumn
  and summer and spring...
In short, *God Is Every*
  Real, Wonderful Thing...
I wish I might meet *Him*
  much more than I do...
I would if there were
  more people like you.

"WHY SHOULD HE DIE
FOR SUCH AS I"

In everything both great and small
We see the Hand of God in all,
And in the miracles of Spring
When *everywhere* in *everything*
His handiwork is all around
And every lovely sight and sound
Proclaims the God of earth and sky
I ask myself *"Just Who Am I"*
That God should send His only Son
That my salvation would be won
Upon a *cross* by a sinless man
To bring fulfillment to God's Plan—
For Jesus suffered, bled and died
That sinners might be sanctified,
And to grant God's children *such as I*
Eternal life in that *Home* on *High.*

THE SEASONS OF THE SOUL

Why am I cast down
        and despondently sad
When I long to be happy
        and joyous and glad?
Why is my heart heavy
        with unfathomable weight
As I try to escape
        this soul-saddened state?
I ask myself often—
        "What makes life this way,
Why is the song silenced
        in the heart that was gay?"
And then with God's help
        it all becomes clear,
The *Soul* has its *Seasons*
        just the same as the year—
I too must pass through
        life's autumn of dying,
A desolate period
        of heart-hurt and crying,
Followed by winter
        in whose frostbitten hand
My heart is as frozen
        as the snow-covered land—
Yes, man too must pass
        through the seasons God sends,

Content in the knowledge
    that everything ends,
And oh what a blessing
    to know there are reasons
And to find that our soul
    must, too, have its seasons—
Bounteous Seasons
    and *Barren Ones,* too,
Times for rejoicing
    and times to be blue,
But meeting these seasons
    of dark desolation
With strength that is born
    of anticipation
That comes from knowing
    that "autumn-time sadness"
Will surely be followed
    by a "Springtime of Gladness."

"I AM THE LIGHT OF THE WORLD"

Oh Father, up in heaven,
      We have wandered far away
From Jesus Christ, Our Saviour,
      Who arose on Easter Day...
And the promise of salvation
      That God gave us when Christ died
We have often vaguely questioned,
      Even doubted and denied...
We've forgotten why You sent us
      Jesus Christ Your Only Son,
And in arrogance and ignorance —
      It's *Our Will,* not *Thine, Be Done* ...
Oh, shed *Thy Light* upon us
      As Easter dawns this year,
And may we feel *The Presence*
      Of the *Risen Saviour* near...
And, God, in Thy great wisdom,
      Lead us in the way that's right,
And may *"The Darkness"* of this world
      Be conquered by *"Thy Light."*

SPRING SONG

"The earth is the Lord's
     and the fulness thereof"—
It speaks of His greatness
     and it sings of His love,
And the wonder and glory
     of the first Easter morn,
Like the first Christmas night
     when the Saviour was born,
Are blended together
     in symphonic splendor
And God with a voice
     that is gentle and tender
Speaks to all hearts
     attuned to His voice,
Bidding His listeners
     to gladly rejoice...
For He who was born
     to be crucified
Arose from the grave
     to be glorified...
And the birds in the trees
     and the flowers of Spring
All join in proclaiming
     this heavenly King.

IN THE GARDEN OF
GETHSEMANE

Before the dawn of Easter
     There came Gethsemane...
Before the Resurrection
     There were hours of agony...
For there can be no crown of stars
     Without a cross to bear,
And there is no salvation
     Without *Faith* and *Love* and *Prayer,*
And when we take our needs to God
     Let us pray as did His Son
That dark night in Gethsemane—
     "Thy Will, Not Mine, Be Done."

"I KNOW THAT MY REDEEMER LIVETH"

They asked me how I know it's true
That the Saviour lived and died...
And if I believe the story
That the Lord was crucified?
And I have so many answers
To prove His Holy Being,
Answers that are everywhere
Within the realm of seeing...
The leaves that fell at autumn
And were buried in the sod
Now budding on the tree boughs
To lift their arms to God...
The flowers that were covered
And entombed beneath the snow
Pushing through the "darkness"
To bid the Spring "hello"...
On every side Great Nature
Retells the Easter Story—
So who am I to question
"The Resurrection Glory?"

A THANKFUL HEART

Take nothing for granted,
      for whenever you do
The "joy of enjoying"
      is lessened for you—
For we rob our own lives
      much more than we know
When we fail to respond
      or in any way show
Our thanks for the blessings
      that daily are ours...
The warmth of the sun,
      the fragrance of flowers,
The beauty of twilight,
      the freshness of dawn,
The coolness of dew
      on a green velvet lawn,
The kind little deeds
      so thoughtfully done,
The favours of friends
      and the love that someone
Unselfishly gives us
      in a myriad of ways,

Expecting no payment
      and no words of praise—
Oh, great is our loss
      when we no longer find
A thankful response
      to things of this kind,
For the *joy of enjoying*
      and the *Fullness of living*
Are found in the heart
      that is filled with *Thanksgiving.*

THANK YOU, GOD, FOR EVERYTHING

Thank you, God, for everything—
    the big things and the small,
For "every good gift comes from God"—
    the giver of them all—
And all too often we accept
    without any thanks or praise
The gifts God sends as blessings
    each day in many ways,
And so at this *Thanksgiving time*
    we offer up a prayer
To thank you, God, for giving us
    a lot more than our share...
First, thank you for the little things
    that often come our way,
The things we take for granted
    but don't mention when we pray,
The unexpected courtesy,
    the thoughtful, kindly deed,
A hand reached out to help us
    in the time of sudden need...
Oh, make us more aware, dear God,
    of little daily graces
That come to us with "sweet surprise"
    from never-dreamed-of places—

Then, thank you for the *"Miracles"*
       we are much too blind to see,
And give us new awareness
       of our many gifts from Thee,
And help us to remember
       that the *Key* to *Life* and *Living*
Is to make each prayer a *Prayer of Thanks*
       and every day *Thanksgiving.*

THE PRICELESS GIFT OF
CHRISTMAS

Now Christmas is a season
      for joy and merrymaking,
A time for gifts and presents,
      for giving and for taking...
A festive, friendly happy time
      when everyone is gay—
But have we ever really felt
      the *greatness of the day*...
For through the centuries the world
      has wandered far away
From the beauty and the meaning
      of the *Holy Christmas Day*...
For Christmas is a heavenly gift
      that only God can give,
It's ours just for the asking,
      for as long as we shall live...
It can't be bought or bartered,
      it can't be won or sold,
It doesn't cost a penny
      and it's worth far more than gold...
It isn't bright and gleaming
      for eager eyes to see,
It can't be wrapped in tinsel
      or placed beneath a tree...
It isn't soft and shimmering
      for reaching hands to touch,

Or some expensive luxury
　　　　you've wanted very much ...
For the *priceless Gift of Christmas*
　　　　is meant just for the heart
And we receive it only
　　　　when we become a part
Of the kingdom and the glory
　　　　which is ours to freely take,
For God sent the Holy Christ Child
　　　　at Christmas for our sake,
So man might come to know *Him*
　　　　and feel *His Presence* near
And see the many miracles
　　　　performed while *He* was here ...
And this *priceless Gift of Christmas*
　　　　is within the reach of all,
The rich, the poor, the young and old
　　　　the greatest and the small ...
So take *His Priceless Gift of Love,*
　　　　reach out and you receive,
And the only payment that God asks
　　　　is just that *you believe.*

LET US PRAY ON THIS HOLY CHRISTMAS DAY

What better time
And what better season,
What greater occasion
Or more wonderful reason
To kneel down in prayer
And lift our hands high
To the God of creation
Who made land and sky...
And, oh, what a privilege
As the New Year begins
To ask God to wipe out
Our errors and sins
And to know when we ask,
If we are sincere,
He will wipe our slate clean
As we start a New Year...
So at this glad season
When joy's everywhere,
Let us meet Our Redeemer
At the *Altar* of *Prayer.*

FAITH IS A MIGHTY FORTRESS

We stand once more at the end of the year
With mixed emotions of *hope and fear,*
Hope for *the Peace* we long have sought,
Fear that *our hopes* will come to naught...
Unwilling to trust in the *Father's Will,*
We count on our logic and shallow skill
And, in our arrogance and pride,
Man is no longer satisfied
To place his confidence and love
With *Childlike Faith* in God above...
But tiny hands and tousled heads
That kneel in prayer by little beds
Are closer to the dear Lord's heart
And of His Kingdom more a part
Than we who search and never find
The answers to our questioning mind,
For faith in things we cannot see
Requires a child's simplicity...
Oh, Father, grant once more to men
A simple *Childlike Faith* again,
Forgetting *colour, race* and *creed*
And seeing only the heart's deep need...
For *Faith* alone can save man's soul
And lead him to a *higher goal,*
For there's but one unfailing course—
We win by *Faith* and *not* by *Force.*

AFTER THE WINTER...GOD
SENDS THE SPRING

Springtime is a season
      Of Hope and Joy and Cheer,
There's beauty all around us
      To see and touch and hear...
So, no matter how downhearted
      And discouraged we may be,
New Hope is born when we behold
      Leaves budding on a tree...
Or when we see a timid flower
      Push through the frozen sod
And open wide in glad surprise
      Its petaled eyes to God...
For this is just God saying—
      "Lift up your eyes to Me,
And the bleakness of your spirit,
      Like the budding springtime tree,
Will lose its wintry darkness
      And your heavy heart will sing"—
For God never sends The Winter
      Without the Joy of Spring.

MY THANKS!

People everywhere in life
  from every walk and station,
From every town and city
  and every state and nation
Have given me so many things
  intangible and dear,
I couldn't begin to count them all
  or even make them clear...
I only know I owe so much
  to people everywhere
And when I put my thoughts in verse
  it's just a way to share
The musings of a thankful heart,
  a heart much like your own,
For nothing that I think or write
  is mine and mine alone...
So if you found some beauty
  in any word or line,
It's just "Your Soul's Reflection"
  in "Proximity with Mine."

HELEN STEINER RICE